THE ESSENTIAL 4

HOW TO EFFECTIVELY LEAD YOUR CLIENT TO TAKE CONTROL OF THEIR STATE, THEIR LIFE & THEIR FUTURE

THE TRAINING MANUAL FOR HYPNOTHERAPISTS

Randi Light
Enlightened Living Hypnosis, Inc.
Copyright © 2015

Copyright © 2015 by Randi Light

All rights reserved. This book or any portion thereof may not be reproduced or used in any manner whatsoever without the express written permission of the publisher except for the use of brief quotations in a book review or scholarly journal.

Third printing 2021

ISBN 978-1-943846-12-2

Published by Enlightened Living Hypnosis, Inc.
37 Shore Drive
Portage, IN 46368

www.RandiLightHypnosis.com

Ordering Information:

For information on training for Randi Light's Essential 4 Protocol, visit:

www.RandiLight.org/HypnosisTraining

Special rates are available on quantity purchases by corporations, associations, educators, and others. For details, contact the publisher at the above listed address.

U.S. trade bookstores and wholesalers: please contact Enlightened Living Hypnosis, Inc. at (219) 929-8726 or email randilight@gmail.com.

DEDICATION

This book is dedicated to you, the Healer.

You are an integral part in moving humanity forward into love.

May this manual guide you in your journey of transforming lives.

Table of Contents

Acknowledgments 1

Foreword 3

Preface 5

Introduction 7

The Essential 4™ at a Glance 9

SESSION I The Stress Relief & Confidence Building Session 15

The Stress Relief & Confidence Building Session – Outline 16

The Stress Relief & Confidence Building Session – Tips & Checklist for Success 19

The Stress Relief & Confidence Building Session – Script 22

SESSION II The Regression to the Root Cause 35

The Regression to the Root Cause Session – Outline 36

The Regression to the Root Cause Session – Tips & Checklist for Success 41

The Regression to the Root Cause Session – Script 46

SESSION III The Time Line Therapy Session 53

The Time Line Therapy Session – Outline – Part I 54

The Time Line Therapy Session – Outline – Part II 57

The Time Line Therapy Session – Tips & Checklist for Success 60

The Time Line Therapy Session – Script 63

SESSION IV The Forgiveness Fire™ Session 69

The Forgiveness Fire™ Session – Outline 70

The Forgiveness Fire™ Session – Tips & Checklist for Success 72

The Forgiveness Fire™ Session – Script 74

Positive & Negative Feelings, Emotions, and Beliefs 85

The HeartMath Breathing Technique 87

The Ho'oponopono Prayer 88

Acknowledgments

The Essential 4 is a compilation of many brilliant minds I've had the opportunity to learn from over the years. Here are just a few of the Hypnotists whom I am forever grateful to: Tim Shurr, Gary Rodriquez, Cal Banyan, Debbie Papadakis, Shelley Stockwell Nicholas, Dr. Sharon Forest... and countless others I've encountered on the path.

This manual would not even be close to completion if it wasn't for the persistence of my assistant, Barbara Caine, and editor, Jessica Klemz. You can pay people to do things for you, but there was something magical and empowering when I could feel their love and joy while working on this project. Barbara's enthusiasm and dedication was contagious, and a great energy to keep everyone motivated and on track.

I am grateful to my friends Debra Fleeger, Jerry Savel and Mike Webber. Their support, wisdom and kindness holds me up and keeps me moving forward.

May you be blessed with all that you love and desire.

Foreword

By Shelley Stockwell-Nicholas, PhD
President, The International Hypnosis Federation

Randi Light illuminates what it takes to be here now and let the past go.

Her step-by-step system, The Essential 4™, calls upon hypnosis, guided imagery, sub-personality and NLP (Neuro-Linguistic Programming) so you, and those you help, may blossom in free and expressive profusion...

As a skilled gardener of the mind, she invites you to remove weeds of self-deception and limits, confidently replacing them with seeds of love, joy and celebration. Her ideas grow on you. So read on and in-joy and out-joy...

Preface

When working with a client do you truly believe in them, and their ability to change and heal? Can you actually see their inner beauty and love? Take a moment to think about a time when somebody believed in you beyond something you thought you were capable of doing. Remember how amazing that felt, and how much easier it was for you to step into that role?

Do the same thing with your clients. Believe in them and their ability to transform. It's easier than you think. To start, be an active and compassionate listener. Then hold the space for your client to become the person they want to be. Begin by picturing your client thinner, healthier, happier, stronger, etc. But it goes beyond visualization; you have to feel it in your heart, your mind and your bones. In essence, you need to 'love' your client.

Believing in your client and believing in yourself go together hand in hand. Everyone has fear. Famous, talented performers like Barbara Streisand felt fear but performed anyway. Thankfully, she found a way to rise above the fear and share her gifts. You have special gifts, different than mine, allowing you to be of service to the world. It is crucial for you to breakthrough your fears, recognize your gifts, and use them every day for your clients and for humanity.

Do you put yourself into a resourceful state before working with a client? I do. I believe it creates confidence in my clients and myself. Resourceful means ingenious and enterprising. When you are in resourceful state, you are more focused, and it's easier to trust your intuition. I suggest that you make it a priority to get yourself into a resourceful state before you begin each session. The words, ideas and answers you need will flow through you and help your clients get even better and results and be even more successful.

One way of getting yourself into a resourceful state before your client shows up is to do a rapid self-hypnosis process. I ask for guidance in the session, for both the client and for myself. Remember to imagine your client exactly how they want to be.

The Essential 4 Training Manual can be used with or without the 5-day training. Personally, I love getting trained in highly effective and fast techniques for change. If you are reading this you are most likely intuitive and can still increase your success rates by incorporating the insights found in this book.

With Love (and Light)
Randi Light

Introduction

The Essential 4™ came together after years of working with clients and personally being trained by many 'Masters.' I also noticed that some clients were only willing to invest in smaller packages so I asked myself, *"If my clients are only willing to invest in four sessions, what can I do during those four sessions that would be the most beneficial and get them the fastest results?"* The Essential 4 is a compilation of the most transformational sessions. I truly believe that almost every person on the planet would benefit from going through The Essential 4™

When I began my journey as a hypnotherapist, I knew that regression was extremely important, but I felt uncomfortable doing it on the first session for a number of reasons. Also, some people, like myself, are called analyzer / resistors and regression can be difficult for us. Furthermore, some clients were so emotionally distraught by the time they got to my office that I realized I needed to first build them up emotionally, reduce their stress, and teach (or re-teach) them how to respond resourcefully to the world around them.

The *Stress Relief & Confidence Building Session* was born. It is designed to generate 'fertile ground' filled with peace, confidence, and self-love. Its purpose is to teach clients how to think and begin the journey of emotional clearing in a light, easy and creative way. As our clients rediscover their confidence, best qualities, and how to respond more resourcefully, we are preparing them for the deeper regression work in which emotional clearing of negative emotions and limiting beliefs can occur.

With the groundwork done, most clients are ready for the *Regression to the Root Cause Session*. I truly believe regression is the cornerstone of success as it provides an opportunity for deep healing and transformation to take place on the cellular level. The client heals their history, reframing their experiences and their future.

The *Time line Therapy Session* continues the journey of emotional clearing. It's a unique, fast, and dissociative approach to regression. The client releases and transforms a dominant limiting belief, allowing your client to get to show up as their best self.

Furthermore, the process of discovery of how one maps and codes time, along with setting it up resourcefully, is a game-changer for many people. Additionally, many clients have painful memories right in front of their faces, which can easily be moved out of the way or 'blasted' right out of their time line. As a result, the client feels better about themselves and their future and is well on their way to creating a bright and compelling one.

Confidence building, healing their history, and emotional clearing all pave the way for *The Forgiveness Fire™ Session*. I believe forgiveness is key because it helps to let go of the pain so healing can take place. In essence, all the confidence building and 'weed pulling' is preparation for the ultimate healing opportunity — forgiveness and acceptance.

I believe it is imperative to include these sessions with almost every client walking through your door. The Essential 4™ sessions are designed to be cumulative and sequential. The results have been beyond my wildest expectations, and it's with great pleasure I share them with you.

The Essential 4™ at a Glance

I. The Stress Relief & Confidence Building Session

1. Induction with Convincers

2. Positive Suggestions

    a. "Focus on what you want, what you like, what you can do and what you could feel truly grateful for."

    b. "You are / feel so much more calm, confident and in control of your thoughts, feelings, actions and reactions."

    c. "Become the Observer instead of the Judge."

3. Guide client to the Room of their Subconscious Mind, the Center of their Being.

    a. "Become aware of all the positive feelings, emotions and beliefs, and the negative feelings, emotions and beliefs."

    b. "Focus on and feel all the positive feelings (State them one at a time.)

    c. "Release / let go of each negative feeling, one by one and throw them in a hole that is now opening up in the room of your subconscious mind."

    d. "White light / positive feelings grow and expand, filling the places and spaces where negative feelings used to be with positivity."

    e. "Inhale security and purity, the white light and all the positive feelings until filled up."

4. Install the 4 L's: Learn, Laugh, Let it go, and Love yourself.

5. Take client out of hypnosis.

II. The Regression to the Root Cause Session

1. "What went well? What can we celebrate?" Coach your client.

2. Induction with convincers

3. Positive suggestions

    a. Ego strengthening, confidence building, including information from pre-talk and intake form

4. "Choose a recent memory when you felt the negative feeling."

5. "Relive that memory — become aware of thoughts, feelings and beliefs."

6. "Follow the feeling back to the root cause."

7. B.E.R.P. your client so the memory becomes neutral or empowering. Beliefs, Emotions, Resources, Positive Learnings.

    a. Love and snuggle.

    b. Rescue.

    c. Play a song.

    d. Give them resources.

    e. Do EFT with a Guarantee. (Emotional Freedom Technique — Tapping process)

    f. Have the client state the *Ho'oponopono Prayer*.

    g. Change submodalities.

    h. Change the belief to the truth.

    i. Change the event.

    j. Ask client to shrink younger self and put in heart to love and protect.

8. "Move forward in time, healing, integrating and re-evaluating all the memories connected." This is called a quantum healing.

9. Future pace at 1 month and 6 months — discover resources, get message and merge.

III. THE TIME LINE THERAPY WITH REGRESSION TO DOMINANT LIMITING BELIEF SESSION (PARTS I AND II)

1. Discuss and uncover the client's dominant limiting belief.

2. Explain Time Line and the mapping and coding of past, present and future memories.

3. Learn how client maps and codes time.
    a. Start with past memories.
    b. Get about 4–5 neutral, past memory markers.
    c. Get about 4–5 neutral, future memory markers.

4. Have client determine if there are more resourceful/useful ways of mapping and coding time to help them be the best they can be.

5. Have them use their hands, bodies and visualizations to relocate time.

6. Check to see if the change makes the client feel lighter or tighter. Keep updating the timeline until the client feels lighter in their belly or chest.

7. Prepare client for hypnosis.
    a. Induction

THE ESSENTIAL 4: HOW TO EFFECTIVELY LEAD YOUR CLIENT TO TAKE CONTROL OF THEIR STATE, THEIR FUTURE & THEIR LIFE

    b. Have client ask higher self or subconscious mind to become aware of the dominant limiting belief that they are to release today.

    c. Rise above body and time lines becoming the Observer.

    d. Ask for a guide to travel back in time with them.

    e. Go back in time to the root cause of the limiting belief.

    f. Client becomes aware of and preserves positive learnings.

    g. Client travels back in time until the emotions become neutralized.

    h. Client comes back to now, and again, you check to see if the emotions are neutralized.

    i. Fill the client up with positive resources as colors and symbols. And have those resources as colors and symbols flow through the timeline.

    j. Then merge with client of today.

IV. THE FORGIVENESS FIRE™ SESSION

1. Prepare the client: explain the what, where and how of Forgiveness Fire™ Session

2. Ask client and write down answers:

    a. *"What do you think forgiveness is?"* and

    b. *"What do you think forgiveness does?"*

    c. Use these answers at the Forgiveness Fire™ session.

3. Induction with intentions

4. Invite a guide to go with them to The Forgiveness Fire™.

5. Bring the client to the entrance of the Welcoming Woods / Friendly Forest.

6. Utilize *HeartMath Breathing Technique* to open their heart.

7. Journey through the woods to the meadow where the Forgiveness Fire™ lives.

8. Forgiveness suggestions — including what the client initially said about forgiveness.

9. Invite 1st person (or people) they need to forgive, or be forgiven, including self.

    a. Client welcomes person and begins communication from the heart.

    b. Person responds to what was said, and also communicates, until everything that needs to be said and done is said and done by all present.

10. Check for cords connecting your client to the person who came to the Forgiveness Fire™.

    a. Discover where each cord is coming out of the body and where it's going. (*Do not check for cords if it's a part of themselves*).

    b. Get specifics on the cords — size, shape, color, thickness, flowing, or stagnate or both?

    c. Give your client the choice to:

    - Sever the cord(s) and take back soul fragments and power.
    - Relocate the cord(s) — heart to heart.

- Sever and create new cord, heart to heart from and with the Creator.
- Recite the *Ho'oponopono Prayer* to your client so that the client can say it to the person who came and vice versa.

11. Future pace — Visualize and feel the evidence of the changes. Get a message, Merge.

12. Take client out of hypnosis.

SESSION I

THE STRESS RELIEF & CONFIDENCE BUILDING SESSION

"To Love thyself is to love and thank all of existence…"

—*Dr. Masaru Emoto*

The Stress Relief & Confidence Building Session
— Outline —

1. Induction with Convincers

2. Suggestions — "From now on, from this moment forward..."

    a. "You are feeling calm, confident and in control. In control of your thoughts, feelings, actions and reactions."

    b. "Focus on what you want, what you like, what you can do and feel grateful for."

    c. "Become the Observer instead of the Judge."

3. Take clients to the Room of their Subconscious Mind; the Center of their Being.

4. "Become aware of positive and negative feelings stored in the room of your subconscious."

    a. "Perhaps all the positive feelings are stored on white post-it notes or something similar and the negative feelings are stored on colored post-its, or something similar."

5. Focus on, and say, each positive feeling, emotion and belief.

6. You might be ahead of me, or I might be ahead of you, and that's okay because you'll catch up with me or I'll catch up with you."

7. One at a time, state all the positive feelings and beliefs that could be stored in the room — love, peace, strength, confidence, curiosity, courage, etc. *As the hypnotist, I have a piece of paper with positive and negative feelings written on it, to remember to say them all.*

8. Have clients breathe each positive feeling into their hearts, and into their very cells — state the positive feelings as suggestions.

9. Have the client focus on releasing and letting go of the negative feelings, emotions and beliefs.

    a. "Imagine a hole opening up in the room of your subconscious mind that can burn, suck out or shred negative feelings, emotions, and beliefs."

    b. "One at a time, pull off, crumble up and dispose of the negative feelings."

    c. Repeat how good it feels to release the negative feelings and the **hold** they have had on their mind, body and life and their past, present and future.

10. "Imagine the positive feelings growing and expanding into this beautiful white light filling all the places and spaces where the negative feelings used to be with positivity."

11. The hole closes; negative feelings are sucked out.

12. The white light forms a bubble, a shield — the white light of protection around the client.

    a. Have the client breathe the positive feelings in, so the white light is around and inside of them, until the client is completely filled up with the white light and all its positivity and all the positive feelings of love, strength, courage, trust, peace, confidence, etc.

13. The Room dissolves.

    a. "Imagine the room dissolving now, but the protective and loving white light surrounds you like a shield, a bubble, or blanket, and it is growing inside of you with every breath you take, until you are filled up with the white light, and all the positive feelings, emotions, and beliefs."

    b. "Breathe in love, strength, courage, peace, trust, and confidence, until you are completely filled up with the white light and all the positive feelings.

THE ESSENTIAL 4: HOW TO EFFECTIVELY LEAD YOUR CLIENT TO TAKE CONTROL OF THEIR STATE, THEIR FUTURE & THEIR LIFE

14. Install the 4 L's — Learn, Laugh, Let it go, and Love yourself by having clients imagining themselves in 1 or 2 different situations in their future utilizing each strategy.

    a. Learn — Ask yourself, "What can I learn from this?"

    b. Laugh — "Laugh at things that used to bother you."
        — "See the humor you couldn't see before."
        — Laugh with them and use 'happy pills' to play laughing sounds.

    c. Let things go — "Let negative thoughts, feelings, and events go."
        — "Become like Harry Potter or Hermione and pluck that negative thought out of your head or your body and throw it behind you."
        — Have them imagine a heavy backpack sliding off their shoulders and down their back as they let it go.

    d. Love yourself — Use the HeartMath breathing technique.
        — "Breathe in love and out love so love is in you and surrounding you."
        — "Invite your heart to open and see, hear and feel your heart open like a rosebud opening into a beautiful rose or a door opening, tunnel flowing or vortex spinning."
        — "Time travel back in time to a loving memory to relive it and feel that loving feeling..." "This is who you really are, love, unconditional love, universal love..."
        — "Make a commitment to love and accept yourself just the way you are. To become your own BFF, Best Friend Forever."
        — "I have a gift for you. It's a bracelet and it works like this..."

12. Take client out of hypnosis.

THE STRESS RELIEF & CONFIDENCE BUILDING SESSION
– TIPS & CHECKLIST FOR SUCCESS –

BEFORE HYPNOSIS:

- ☐ Plan at least 1½ to 2 hours for the 1st session and pre-talk.

- ☐ Determine if the client is ready to do emotional clearing and enter the Room of the Subconscious. Most of the time, the client is ready. If not, do everything but the emotional clearing. (If they are super stressed, anxious or in the middle of a divorce or other type of difficulty, it's probably best to take them to the Room on the 2nd session.

- ☐ Have the client read and sign an agreement that includes a promise to stop self-criticism and become their own BFF (Best Friend Forever).

- ☐ Include an educational, scientific, and experiential pre-talk.

- ☐ Encourage the client to have a great hypnotic experience by letting them know, *"Your mind is the creative mind and knows how to help you be the best you can be."*

DURING HYPNOSIS:

- ☐ Create and use your list of positive feelings, emotions and beliefs, and negative feelings, emotions, and beliefs to state while in the Room of the Subconscious. Remember it's fine to group similar emotions together.

- ☐ Since there are numerous positive feelings, you can group some of them together and skip others. Just make sure to reinforce, emphasize and include what your clients are coming in for.

THE ESSENTIAL 4: HOW TO EFFECTIVELY LEAD YOUR CLIENT TO TAKE CONTROL OF THEIR STATE, THEIR FUTURE & THEIR LIFE

- ☐ You can also add suggestions in the Room of the Subconscious (and other places) to include:
    - Weight Loss — *From now on, you naturally feel more capable to take off that weight.*
    - Confidence — *You naturally feel more confident to become the best version of yourself.*

- ☐ When deciding on the order you state the feelings, make sure to start with resourceful ones that you know your client has experienced.
    - Love, Peace, Courage, Strength, Confidence, Trust, Caring, Compassion, Forgiveness, Joy, Patience, Happiness, Capable, Determined, Motivated, Driven, Spiritual, Connected, Empowered, Powerful. You are enough, good enough, loved enough, strong enough, creative enough, etc.
    - Frustration, Worry, Doubt, Anger, Resentment, Fear, Pain, Rejection, Regret, Guilt, Defeat, etc.

- ☐ Continuously make sure the client is still with you and doing the things you are asking. If client goes too deep, have them say, "yes" out loud instead of just having them nod their head in response to your questions.

- ☐ During the 2nd L — Laughing at things: Use your voice to laugh as well as a 'Hypnotic Enhancer' by playing giggling sounds at the same time you are future pacing the client so they automatically laugh at things that used to bother them.
    - Use a laughing babies soundtrack.
    - Use a happy pill plush toy that makes giggling sounds when you press it.

THE ESSENTIAL 4: HOW TO EFFECTIVELY LEAD YOUR CLIENT TO TAKE CONTROL OF THEIR STATE, THEIR FUTURE & THEIR LIFE

- ☐ Gift the client a bracelet to remind them to speak positively about themselves and their lives. For example, I gift the bracelet during the LOVING YOURSELF component of the 4 L's. The bracelet reminds them to immediately change negative statements to positive statements and then switch the bracelet to the other wrist. The goal is to stop self-criticism.

Contact Randi Light to order 'Enlightened Living' Bracelets to give to your clients.

AFTER HYPNOSIS:

- ☐ Client receives at least 1 hypnosis reinforcement audio program to listen to daily.
    - ○ *You or your client can record the session.*
    - ○ *Or contact Randi Light to order hypnosis audios with a licensing agreement for you to give away to your clients. Confidence, Sleep, Healing, Weight Loss, Peak Performance, Stop Smoking.*

- ☐ Client receives an educational workbook to keep track of their learnings.

Contact Randi Light to order your personalized Guidebooks to give to your clients.

- ➢ *Step Into Your Power,* and
- ➢ *It's Time to Take Off Weight, Feel Great and Keep It Off! – A Journey to Your Best Self*

- ☐ Offer the client a hypnosis magazine and /or a summation of scientific data and research.

- ☐ Client is presented with homework and suggested readings. I recommend and use *You Can Heal Your Life* by Louise Hay, book/DVD set.

The Stress Relief & Confidence Building Session
— Script —

Begin with your favorite Induction or count backwards from 20/10 down to 1 and include a progressive relaxation — Imagine a soothing, healing, relaxing energy flowing into the top of your head... Go through the entire body.

As a result of this deep hypnotic rest, you are going to sleep so much better and feel so much better about yourself and your life. Imagine yourself leaving here today with a wonderful feeling of wellbeing (*include how the emotion the want to feel*) and that wonderful feeling staying with you through the rest of the day and into the evening. Now imagine yourself falling asleep tonight easily and quickly and sleeping peacefully through the night. If you were to wake up, imagine yourself falling back to sleep easily and quickly and then picture yourself waking up in the morning absolutely refreshed and alert and ready to start your day in a whole new way. When you have imagined all of that nod your head.

From now on, from this moment forward, you are and you feel so much more calm, so much more confident, and so much more in control — in control of your thoughts, in control of your feelings, in control of your actions, and reactions.

From now on, from this moment forward, it just gets easier and easier for you to focus your thoughts on what you want, instead of what you don't want... You, from this moment forward have a natural ability to focus on, think about and dwell upon what you want... what you want to experience, what you want more of in your life, what you want instead of what you don't want. Your subconscious and conscious mind now work together, and you naturally focus and dwell upon what you want instead of what you don't want... (*Add suggestions of things you know they want.*)

And from now on, from this moment forward, your subconscious and conscious mind work together to help you focus on what you like instead of what you don't like. It's just easier and easier for you to focus on, think about and dwell upon what you like, what you like about yourself, what you like about your family, what you like about your job, your body and your life.

And from now on, from this moment forward, you also have a natural ability to focus on what you can do, instead of what you can't do. You become even more resourceful than before and focus on what you can do by asking yourself resources questions like, 'What can I do about this?' "What can I do about this?" It will just be easier and easier for you to be more resourceful, ask yourself resourceful questions, and focus on what you can do. From this moment forward, it's a natural habit for you to ask yourself, 'What can I do about this?' And then your subconscious and conscious mind work together and you naturally focus on what you can do.

Also, from this moment forward you have a natural habit to focus on, think about, and dwell upon what you **could** feel truly grateful for and feel that appreciation in your heart. From now on, it's just easier and easier for you to get into that attitude of gratitude and focus on what you could feel truly grateful for. As you do you naturally feel that gratitude in your heart.

Every time you go into hypnosis whether at my office, listening to a hypnosis audio recording, practicing self-hypnosis, or any other way, you go into hypnosis faster and easier, the suggestions grow stronger and deeper, and you have more fun, making it so much easier for you to experience life in a more fulfilling way.

It's just getting easier and easier for you now to be and feel so much more calm... so much more confident... and so much more in control. In control of your thoughts, in control of your feelings, and in control of your actions and reactions.

To help ensure your success and help you be the best you can be you are now becoming the observer instead of the judge. Just like you can put that conscious analytical mind aside, you can put that judging self aside and become the observer of your thoughts, the observer of your behaviors and the observer of other people's behaviors. From this moment forward it's just easier and easier for you to be the observer instead of the judge.

THE ESSENTIAL 4: HOW TO EFFECTIVELY LEAD YOUR CLIENT TO TAKE CONTROL OF THEIR STATE, THEIR FUTURE & THEIR LIFE

To help ensure your success even more, it's time for you to go into the Room of your Subconscious Mind, into the Center of your Being. You might imagine it like a round, dome-shaped room, or your creative mind might imagine it some other way. However you imagine it is right for you.

Now you know after our talk today that everything that has ever happened to you is stored in the room of your subconscious. But today you are going to be focusing on all the positive feelings, emotions, and beliefs that are stored there. And today you are going to begin to release the **hold** that the negative feelings have had on your past, present and future as well as your mind, body, and life.

Once you arrive in the Room of your Subconscious Mind, in the Center of your Being, you might notice that all the positive feelings, emotions, and beliefs are stored on white post-it notes, or something similar… and all the negative feelings, emotions, and beliefs are stored on colored post-it notes, or something similar. However you imagine it is the right way for you.

In a moment I am going count backwards from 3 down to 1 and gently snap my fingers. Just allow each number to relax you, and deepen you, and take you deep within, to the Room of your Subconscious Mind, to the Center of your Being. Nod your head when you are ready to go into the Room of your Subconscious Mind, the Center of your Being… Good — 3 double your relaxation 2, even deeper relaxed now, trust your impressions and 1, (*SNAP*) imagine yourself now in the room of your subconscious, in the center of your being.

Become aware of the all the positive feelings, emotions and beliefs that are stored in your room, perhaps on white post-its or something similar. Also, become aware of all the negative feelings stored there perhaps on colored post-its, or something similar.

Right now, focus all of your attention on the positive feelings, emotions and beliefs that are stored there. Imagine yourself walking towards the wall now to get a closer look at all the positive feelings. Now at some point you might be ahead of me, or I might be ahead of you and that's okay because I'll catch up with you or you'll catch up with me.

Go ahead now and become aware of the **love** that is stored there from your past present and future. You might just sense it, or imagine it, as a picture, a memory, a word, a color, a symbol or some other creative way. Any way you are experiencing the love, is right for you. See that love, hear that love and feel that love. Take a deep breath in and breathe that loving feeling into your heart... and into every cell of your entire being so that you recognize and realize you are loved, loving and lovable... Good. When you have done that, nod your head.

Go ahead now and become aware of all the **peace** that is stored there in your mind, body and life... See that peace, feel that peace and breathe the peace into your heart right now, so that from now on you feel more and more peace every day in every way. Smile when you have down that... Wonderful... Each and every time you see, hear and feel the positive feeling, it amplifies and strengthens the feelings... and the neural pathways... allowing you to experience the positive feelings... more and more... every day in every way.

Now become aware of all the **strength** stored in that room. See, hear and feel that strength. Breathe it into you so that from now on you feel stronger and stronger every day in every way. Good... Go ahead now and become aware of all **confidence** stored in your room. Breathe that confidence into you so that from this moment forward you are more and more confident in all areas of your life for the rest of your life. Nod your head when you have done that... Good.

Now become aware of all the **curiosity** stored in that room from your past, present and future. See, hear and feel that curiosity, that childlike playful sense of wonder... and breathe that curiosity into so you are naturally more and more curious every day in every way. Nod your head when you have done that.

Now become aware of all the **trust** that is stored there from your past, present and future. See, hear, and feel the trust and breathe it into so that from now on you trust, you trust yourself, your trust the Universe (God, Higher Self), you trust the process of life... Good.

Begin to sense, feel and experience the **patience** stored in your room... Amplify the patience right now by breathing patience into your heart and into every cell of your entire being... Good. From this moment forward you are and you feel more and more patience.

Now become aware of and feel all the **courage** in that room. Breathe that courage into you so that from this moment forward you are and you feel more and more courageous every day in every way because you realize that courage isn't the absence of fear, it's feeling the fear and doing it anyway. And when you are vulnerable you are courageous. From this moment forward, you are courageous every day in every way.

Now become aware of that **caring, compassionate, forgiving** feeling for self and others. Breathe in and feel the caring, compassionate, forgiving feeling for self and others... breathe it into you... Breathe in all these wonderful positive feelings... Breathe them into your body, mind and spirit.

Now become aware of and experience that **calm, serene, at ease** feeling so that from now on you feel more calm, more serene and more at ease every day in every way. Nod your head when you have done that... Good. Now become aware of and feel that **spiritual, connected** feeling... Breathe that spiritual connected feeling into you so that you naturally feel more connected to yourself, your family and nature. Sense your connection with all that is right now... Nod your head when you have done that.

Now become aware of and breathe in all the **joy** stored in that room. You have had moments of joy. See, hear and feel that joy now, breathe it into you. Activate that joy gene so you naturally feel more and more joy every day in every way.

Good, now become aware of and feel that **capable, determined** feeling. Breathe that capable, determined, **motivated, driven** feeling into you so that you recognize and realize you are capable, you are determined, motivated and driven to be the best version of yourself. Good... very good. Now become aware of and feel that **empowered, powerful** feeling. Breathe that into you so that you naturally feel more empowered and more powerful every day in every way, easily amplifying your personal power.

THE ESSENTIAL 4: HOW TO EFFECTIVELY LEAD YOUR CLIENT TO TAKE CONTROL OF THEIR STATE, THEIR FUTURE & THEIR LIFE

Now become aware of all the positive beliefs that are stored in your past, present and future. You have had moments when you recognized and realized that you are enough. Sense those beliefs there now and tell yourself the truth, **you are enough, you are enough — you're good enough, you're loved enough... you're strong enough... you're smart enough... you're creative enough... you are enough... you are enough.**

Now to amplify all those positive feelings... It's time for you to become aware of and release the **hold** the negative feelings have had on your mind, body and life. It's time for you to step into your power and become your best version of yourself and release the hold these negative feelings have had on your past, present and future.

Go ahead now and become aware of the negative feelings. As you take a closer look at the negative feelings, you realize they are stored on colored post it notes or something similar so all you really need to do is pull off those negative feelings, crumple them up and throw them in a hole that is now opening up in your room where they can be burned or sucked out or shredded. For example, if there is any frustration there, pull it off, crumble it up and throw it in the hole and let that frustration go. (*Make a letting go breath sound as you say this.*) Imagine it getting burned or sucked out or shredded. Sense all that frustration leaving your mind body and life and your past present and future. Nod your head when you have done that. Good.

Become aware now of any doubt in your room. If there's **doubt** there, just pull it off, crumble it up, throw it in the hole and (*releasing breath sound*) let it go... When you have done that nod your head. Wonderful. Now become aware of any **worry** stored in the room. Just pull it off, throw it in the whole and let it go so that any worry that no longer serves you is gone from you past present and future.

If there's any **guilt** there, throw it in the hole and let it go (*sound*). Feel how good it feels to let any guilt that no longer serves you be gone from your past, present and your future as well as your mind, body and life.

Now become aware of any **anger** that is stored in your room. Throw it in the hole and let it go... Nod your head when you have done that.

Become aware of any **anxiety** stored in your room from your past present and future. Go ahead now and pull it off, throw it in the hole and let it go. Any anxiety that no longer serves is you now gone from you past, present, and your future and it's now gone from your mind, body and your life. Nod your head when you have done that.

If there is any **fear** there, release it now. Any fear that no longer serves you is now gone from your past present and your future. If there's any **rejection** stored in there, release it now. If there is any **depression** there, throw it in that hole and let it go. Feel how good it feels to release the depression that no longer serves you, so it is gone from your past present and your future. If there is any **resentment** stored there, release it right now.

Become aware of any **regret**, and free yourself of that negative emotion right now... If there is any **stress** stored there, release all the stress from your past, present, and future... from your mind, your body, and your life. Notice if there are any feelings of **overwhelm** stored in your room and release them as they no longer serve you. If there are any feelings of being **stuck**, let them go right now. If there is any **jealousy**... let it go, release it... **shame**... burn it up now, release it, let that shame go. It no longer serves you.

Now become aware of all the limiting beliefs that are stored in your room. It's time to remove them and tell yourself the truth. Pull the negative beliefs off and throw them in the hole, as you tell yourself the truth, **you are enough, you're good enough... you're loved enough... you are strong enough... you are smart enough... you are creative enough... you are enough.** Good! Let me know when you have done all of that.

Look around the room and make sure all the negative feelings, emotions, and beliefs are gone. Nod your head when you sense they are gone from you past, present and your future as well as your mind, body and your life... Wonderful.

Now become aware of something amazing happening in the room of your subconscious. The center of your being. Those positive feelings are now growing and expanding and filling all the places and spaces where the negative feelings used to be with positivity, until the entire atmosphere of the room is completely changed. That's right... Imagine those positive feelings growing and expanding into this beautiful, powerful protective white light, filling up all the places and spaces where the negative feelings used to be with positivity.

Imagine the white light of positivity is now forming a bubble, a shield around you protecting you, guiding you. The room can dissolve now, but this white light of positivity stays around you, guiding you and protecting you like a powerful shield.

Now begin to imagine you're breathing in this white light into every cell of your entire being, until you are filled up with the white light and all its positivity. Go ahead now and breath in all its strength, courage, confidence, trust, joy, and peace until every cell of your entire being is filled up with this white light of positivity. Breathe it into every cell of your entire being until you sense it's filled up inside you and surrounding you, guiding you and protecting you as a powerful shield. When you've done that, nod your head. Wonderful.

From now on, it will just be easier and easier for you to respond so much more calm, so much more confident and so much more in control, in control of your thoughts, feelings, actions and reactions.

And to insure all of this we are going to install the 4 L's. So that from now on, from this moment forward, it will be natural for you to learn from things, laugh at things, let things go, and love yourself more and more every day.

The 1st L is learning. Imagine it's your future and you have cultivated a new habit of learning from every life experience, especially the ones that used to bother you. Because you now recognize and realized that there is no such thing as failure, only feedback and everything in life can be a learning experience. Imagine right now that you already have this ability to learn from every life experience and that your mind automatically responds with, "What can I learn from this?" and then you learn something from it. You realize when you learn something from it you can let it go, you can move on. You can change what you focus on and how you feel, very quickly, just like that (*SNAP*).

Pick a situation that would have bothered you in some small way in the past, only now your mind automatically responds with 'What can I learn from this? What can I learn from this?" and then you learn something from it, so you let it go, you move on, you change how you feel, very quickly, from a negative state to a positive state, just like that (*SNAP*). Picture yourself, in your future learning something from it and moving on. Nod your head when you have done that... Good.

So, from now on, from this moment forward, your subconscious and conscious mind works together, and you have a natural habit to learn from every life experience by asking yourself the resourceful question, "What can I learn from this?" and then you learn something from it, so you let it go, you move on and change how you feel very quickly, just like that (*SNAP*).

The 2nd L is laughing. Laughing at things that used to bother you. (*Laugh as you deliver this suggestion and periodically as you install this habit.*) From now on, from this moment forward, you have a natural ability to laugh at things (*LAUGH*) to see the humor in your own behaviors, and in other people's behaviors, too. It will just be easier for you now to laugh at it and let it go. And if the Universe gives you exactly what you don't want, you recognize what is going on and you find yourself laughing at the situation and just letting it go and moving on... And as you laugh, you release chemical endorphins that make you feel so much better (*laugh when you are saying this*).

Imagine it's your future, and you have this natural ability to laugh at situations that used bother you. You now realize you can see the humor you couldn't see before. Or perhaps your creative mind imagines you are watching a really funny movie, like *Happy Gilmore*, or maybe you think of a funny comedian, and then you easily and naturally laugh at the situation, and let it go. You move on. You change how feel very quickly from a negative state to a positive state, just like that. (*SNAP*). Then you feel so much better about yourself and your life. Picture yourself in a future situation that would have bothered you a little in the past but you now see the humor in your behaviors and other peoples ridiculous behaviors so you laugh and when you laugh at it, you easily let it go and change how you feel just like that (*SNAP*). (*When they are imagining laughing, I squeeze my little happy pill stuffed animal that makes laughing sounds. You can giggle or play giggling sounds too.*) Nod your head when you have done that... Very good.

The 3rd L is letting things go. From now on, from this moment forward, you subconscious and conscious mind works together, and you easily and quickly learn from things, laugh at things, and let things go that no longer serve you. You let negative thoughts go, negative feelings go, negative people and negative situations go, too.

From this moment forward, you have a natural ability to let things go. Perhaps you can imagine you have a talent like Harry Potter or Hermione, and you can pluck that negative thought or feeling right out of your mind and body. Or maybe you imagine you have a big heavy backpack weighing on your shoulders, and you feel one strap falling off, and then the other strap falling off, and the backpack hits the ground (*CLAP*). You move forward feeling lighter, and freer because you let it go.

In a moment, imagine you already have this natural ability to let things go that used to bother you. Picture a situation that would have bothered you a little in the past only you now have a natural ability to let it go. As you imagine letting it go, feel how good it feels. Use all your senses. Nod your head when you have done that... Good. From now on, from this moment forward, you have a natural ability to learn from things, laugh at things and let things go.

And the 4th L brings it all together, loving yourself. From now on, you are learning to love and accept yourself just the way you are. It begins with you making a promise to stop that old pattern of criticizing yourself. It's time for you to make a commitment to yourself right now to stop being mean to yourself

THE ESSENTIAL 4: HOW TO EFFECTIVELY LEAD YOUR CLIENT TO TAKE CONTROL OF THEIR STATE, THEIR FUTURE & THEIR LIFE

and to become your own best friend to have your own back. Nod your head when you have done that... Good

To make it even easier for you to learn to love and accept, you must awaken your heart's intelligence. It's easy to connect with your heart's intelligence. All you need to do is begin to imagine that you are breathing through your heart right now. That's right, imagine that as you breathe in, you are breathing in through your heart (*say this out loud when they are breathing in*) and as you breathe out, imagine you are breathing out through your heart (*say this out loud when they are breathing out*). It's easy for you to do this. Just focus your attention on your heart.

As you breathe like this, you literally activate your heart's intelligence. Your heart tells your brain what to do more times a day than your brain tells your heart. As you imagine breathing in and out through your heart, imagine you are breathing in and out love, unconditional love, universal love. Imagine you are breathing in and out the color, sounds and feelings of love. Breathing in love and out love so love is in your and surrounding you. To amplify that love, in just a moment, invite your heart to open, and then see, hear, and feel it opening perhaps like a rosebud opening into a beautiful red or purple rose or a door opening, tunnel flowing or vortex spinning. However your creative, wise mind imagines and feels your heart opening is right for you.

Now let's amplify that loving feeling even more by choosing a memory when you felt that feeling. That memory could have been yesterday or many years ago. Very soon indeed you are going to go back in time to an event in your life when you felt very loving, or very loved, or both. It could be a memory of you petting an animal, dancing, holding someone or being held. Choose a time in your life when you felt very loved or very loving or both. When you have chosen that memory, nod your head... Wonderful.

In a moment I am going to count backwards from 3 down to 1, and gently snap my fingers, as I do, allow each number to relax you and deepen you, and take you back in time to that loving memory. You are going to become a time traveler and go back in time to that event and relive it. As you imagine the loving experience, make it big and bright, and lifelike, hear all the sounds and feel all the feelings. If there is skin, feel the skin... if there is fur, feel the fur... and really feel that **wonderful, powerful, loving** feeling, as you step into the scene and relive it over and over. Visualize it so passionately that you can feel the love, and easily breathe that loving feeling into your heart so love is in you and surrounding you.

Nod your head when you are ready. 3, deeper now, use all your senses, 2, traveling back in time to that loving memory and 1 (*SNAP*), be there now and relive the memory over and over. See, hear and feel the love. Amplify it, and breathe the loving feeling into your heart, into every cell of your being... unconditional love, universal love. Recognize that this feeling is the real you. Now make a promise once again, to become your own BFF, to have your back, stop self-criticism and learn to love and accept yourself more and more every in every way. When you have done that nod your head... Wonderful.

> **To help you be the best you can be, I have a gift for you, it's a bracelet. The bracelet works like this. You put the bracelet on your wrist, and the next time you catch yourself saying something negative or critical about yourself, you say, 'STOP' and see a big red stop sign... and then you immediately change your statements to something positive and truthful. That's the most important part. Then, you take the bracelet off your wrist and put it on the other wrist. Then, the next time you catch yourself saying something negative or critical about yourself, or even the world, you say, 'STOP' see a big red stop sign... and you immediately change your statements to something positive and truthful. That's the most important part, and then, you take the bracelet off of your wrist and put it on the other wrist with the goal being to keep the bracelet on the same wrist for up to one day and then eventually one week. If you would like this gift, nod your head (*Or have them turn over their hand and put the bracelet in their hand*).

From now on, from this moment forward, you focus on your positive qualities and your positive characteristics. And you learn to love and accept yourself more and more every day in every way. It is now easy and natural for you to learn from things, laugh at things, let things go and love yourself. This is the new you that is about to emerge.

In a moment I am going to count from 1 up to 5, when I get to 5 a new you will emerge, with new beliefs about yourself, your life and your future. Starting with the count of 1, take a big, energy breath in, 2, speeding up now with lots of confidence and energy, 3, coming up even more, with more confidence and energy, 4, almost there and with the count of 5 (*SNAP*) open your eyes.

SESSION II

THE REGRESSION TO THE ROOT CAUSE

"All that we are is a result of what we have thought."

—The Buddha

"Imagination is the preview of life's coming attractions."

—Albert Einstein

THE REGRESSION TO THE ROOT CAUSE SESSION
— OUTLINE —

> *Regression to cause.*
> *Regression to the root cause.*
> *Regression to the source of the problem.*
> *Regression to the ISE (Initial Sensitizing Event).*
> *Regression to the first time you ever felt that way.*

1. Explain regression to your client:

    a. Include examples of past regressions.

    b. How regression releases the stored emotions and brings an adult understanding into the memories.

    c. Sometimes clients go back to the root cause and sometimes clients will go back in time to a memory that needs healing. This is common but continue going back in time until you get to the root cause.

    d. The Older Self can help that younger self to release the stored emotion from the body, create and update beliefs so that a quantum healing can take place in all the memories connected to the event.

    e. Let them know that they don't have to relive a traumatic scene. Their adult self can rescue that younger self by getting that younger self out of that scene.

    f. Make sure your client is ready for regression. They need to agree to be there for their younger self no matter what happened in that scene!!

    g. You will ask client to remember a recent memory — it could have been yesterday, a few weeks ago, or months ago when they felt that negative feeling.

2. Induction with convincers.

3. Ego strengthening and confidence building suggestions.

4. Have client choose a recent memory when they felt the dominant negative feeling.

    a. "You may have many memories of that negative feeling. It doesn't matter which one you choose, just choose a memory that stands out right now."

5. Take client back to recent memory.

    a. "3, 2, 1 back to that recent memory — trust your impressions, become aware now of your thoughts, feelings and beliefs... heighten your senses, replay the memory — What are you feeling?" "What do you believe?"

    b. "When you communicate with me your voice will keep you very focused on what you need to be focused on."

6. Get them associated and focused on the feeling.

    a. "What are you feeling in this recent scene?"

    b. "Where do you feel it? In your head, heart, belly all over?"

    c. "What shape, size and color? Is it round, square, globular, pointy?" *Remember to give the client ideas.*

7. Explain & do.

    a. Touch their arm and hold it while counting backwards from 3 down to 1 — "Amp up that feeling now, but only as much as you can handle." State the feeling and its shape and color. This makes it come up and out of your body and your subconscious can follow the feeling back to the source to the root cause, to the first time you ever felt that feeling." (It's optional to touch their arm.)

    b. "With the count of 3 amp up that feeling but only as much as you can handle, time traveling back in time. 2, Trust your first impressions traveling back in time to the root cause to the source, and 1, (*SNAP*). Be there now. Trust your impressions. Are you inside or outside…?"

8. Get them associated with the memory to discover feelings and beliefs.

   a. "Are you inside or outside? Daytime or nighttime? Alone or with someone or with people?"

   b. Sometimes I will ask the questions before they answer to get them more associated with the memory.

9. Ask more questions.

   a. "Around what age are you…?

   b. What's happening…?"

   c. "What are you feeling…? If needed ask, "Are you feeling 'scared, mad, happy, frustrated…?"

   d. "What else are you feeling…? What's happening…?"

   e. "What belief did you create as a result of this event…?"

   f. "Is this a new feeling or a familiar feeling for that you…?"

> *Sometimes I will ask questions like this and other times I will tell them, "We will help that younger you in just a moment. But right now, we are going to go back in time, to the source, to the root cause, to the first time you ever felt that feeling."*

10. Familiar Feeling.

    a. "We'll help that younger you in just a moment. We are going to go even farther back in time now to the root cause, to the source of that feeling, 3, amp up that feeling but only as much as you can handle, time traveling back in time to the root cause, to the source, 2, even farther back in time to the source the root cause, and 1, (*SNAP*). Be there now. Are you inside or outside…?"

11. Repeat above until it's a new feeling or the first time they felt that feeling.

12. Once it's a new feeling: "Bring the adult you into that scene now to rescue (get that younger you to a peaceful place) or love up that younger you…"

    RESCUE — "Get that younger you out of that scene now to a safe and peaceful place. Nod your head when you have done that." Or…

    LOVE — "Do whatever you need to do to help that younger you in that scene to feel a better. You might hug, hold and snuggle up that younger you. Talk to her/him and let her know you will always be there…"

    LEARN — Help client become aware of one or more positive things they can learn from this situation.

13. **B.E.R.P.** — BERP your clients in every memory so that the memory becomes emotionally neutral or empowering.

    a. Discover what they **Believe**.

    b. Uncover the **Emotions**.

    c. Give them **Resources** to be downloaded like a superpower to handle the scene differently (Strength, Courage, Love, Confidence, Trust). "Go back in time to right before that scene began. What resources would help you get through that scene so it becomes neutral or empowering."

    d. Take **Positive learnings**.

14. Play a song for them to connect and love younger self. I recommend "You Are So Beautiful" by Joe Cocker.

15. Do anything else that needs to be said or done in that scene to neutralize the emotions and take one or more positive learnings from the experience.

    a. Hug someone.

    b. Speak up for yourself.

    c. Have adult self do something.

d. Make the client really big and the perpetrator really small.

e. Fire a parent and give them a new parent.

16. Have client shrink younger self and put him/her in their heart to be loved and cared for.

17. Move forward in time to the next most important scene. *I usually write down the memories and have the client go through each one to make sure they are feeling good in each of the scenes that came up, as you progress forward to now.*

    a. If feeling better, run through each scene with the scene being neutral or empowering.

    b. If emotion is still strong have adult self drop into scene to assist — do whatever it takes to feel better.

18. Keep moving forward in time through all the scenes discussed until you get into the RECENT scene when you began the regression.

    a. Allow the client to drop into any scene they want to help that younger self to learn, let go and neutralize or empower.

19. Future Pace.

    a. Move forward in time into your future — Imagine 1 month from today

    b. Move forward in time into your future — Imagine 6 months from today.

20. Have the client picture the qualities and resources in that future self. Get wisdom from future self and celebrate. "You are now a team working together."

21. Right before taking your client out of hypnosis, have them put their hands on their heart and tell them to say hello to themselves and also say I love you and their name. Have them repeat this and state 1, 2, or 3 affirmations that reinforces the 'new you' that is about to emerge.

The Regression to the Root Cause Session
— Tips & Checklist for Success —

BEFORE HYPNOSIS:

☐ Ask the client, "What went well for you since the last time I saw you?"

☐ Explain regression. Give specific examples of past regressions and how it helps you move forward and get out of a negative state quickly.

☐ Explain how it works. Your subconscious mind can follow a feeling back to the root cause.

☐ Trust your first impressions — whatever you are sensing could be very important.

☐ Sometimes it's a conscious memory and sometimes it's not — either way the information and or memory has a purpose.

☐ Sometimes it's a representation of a recurring memory (Gestalt).

☐ Explain that they will not have to relive a traumatic memory, but instead their adult self will come in and get that younger you out of that scene.

☐ Be clear which dominant negative emotion the client will be releasing.

☐ Have the client choose a recent memory when they felt that negative feeling.

☐ Let the client know that tears are very common and normal for both men and women.

DURING HYPNOSIS:

☐ Include ego strengthening and confidence building prior to regression.

THE ESSENTIAL 4: HOW TO EFFECTIVELY LEAD YOUR CLIENT TO TAKE CONTROL OF THEIR STATE, THEIR FUTURE & THEIR LIFE

- ☐ Be prepared for Plan B — *Parts Therapy*. If your client doesn't produce a memory, bring in the part that feels that negative feeling.

- ☐ Bring client to a 'peaceful place' first and let them know they can go there anytime during the regression.

- ☐ Give the client ideas or examples for questions: "Is it round, globular, square...? Are you feeling angry, sad, frustrated, happy...?"

AFTER HYPNOSIS:

- ☐ Ask the client how they feel when they come out of hypnosis.

- ☐ Discuss homework to do for next session (from guidebook).

- ☐ Let them know more memories and insights can continue to surface over the next few hours and sometimes days. Encourage them to process kindly towards themselves.

- ☐ They can feel however they want to feel for the day but also let them know that they should start feeling better in the next couple of minutes (if they are emotionally drained).

- ☐ Give them homework from guidebook to go over the belief components.

PREPARING FOR THE UNEXPECTED:

The emotions can change in each memory. That's common. Just have them follow the new feeling back in time, to the source. (Do people ever really know what they are feeling?)

Have your client experience a peaceful place prior to doing regression. Then, if necessary, they have an automatic relaxation option. (Remember that being in hypnosis is a safe place for them to be.)

- ☐ **Client regresses back to a resourceful memory instead of one that needs clearing.**
    - o Utilize this and then move them either forward or backward in time to a scene that needs healing. Basically, just continue doing the regression but with the positive resources awakened.

- ☐ **Client regresses back to a recent memory.**
    - o That's okay, just keep taking the client farther back in time until they get to the root cause.

- ☐ **Sometimes your Subconscious Mind won't allow you to go back to that part of the scene.**
    - o Client says they aren't anywhere or it's dark.
        - — Could be womb — guide them through a womb experience by cleaning up the womb.
        - — Could be fear / not ready to go through the memory / etc.
    - o If you can't get them associated with a memory do PARTS THERAPY instead. Invite the part of them that makes them feel — angry, guilty, sad, etc.

- ☐ **Spontaneous Past Life Regression.**
    - o Consider treating it just as you would a regular regression.
    - o Or you may need to take them through that lifetime as you would a PAST LIFE REGRESSION SESSION.

Sometimes the client doesn't understand and automatically goes back in time to the root cause instead of a recent memory — go with it!

- **Regression with Children.**
    - I do the regular regression techniques with young adults ages 15 & up.
    - With younger children I will do regression but handle it differently than with adults. Many times, younger children won't understand, but you can guide them in a number of ways:
        - Go through various younger ages starting when 1 year old or older.
        - If you know of a specific event from the intake, take them to it and help them reframe that event. B.E.R.P. them.
        - Make sure the children feel empowered, safe and loved by:
            - Getting them out of where they are.
            - Bringing in pets; God; their favorite superhero, parents; angels; spirit guides; cartoon characters; you, the hypnotist… Use anything and everything that fits their belief systems.
            - Empower them with these ideas:
                - Big plexiglass shields
                - Superpowers
                - Change the submodalities
                    - Make it funny with top hats or silly-looking spiders.
                    - They get really big & someone else gets as small as an ant.

- **Sleep Issues with Regression.**
    - Consciously but with eyes closed, have client imagine going through an evening they didn't sleep well — hour by hour, starting from getting ready for bed and asking them what they are thinking, feeling and believing.
    - Then take them into hypnosis to that same evening and regress them back to the first emotion that showed up.

- Next, move them forward in time to the evening when their sleep was disturbed and check hour by hour if they are sleeping now.

☐ **Virtual Regressions.**
- Be clear on what you feel comfortable with — establish boundaries.
- Things to consider discussing before the session:
  - Creating a peaceful place for them to go to.
  - Request that someone else is home to assist, just in case.
  - The level of rapport you have with the client.
  - Client's previous experiences with hypnosis.
  - Age of client.
  - Computer plugged in vs. using the battery.
  - Phone on or off.

THE REGRESSION TO THE ROOT CAUSE SESSION
— SCRIPT —

> *Include ego strengthening and confidence building suggestions at the beginning based on intake form and previous sessions with client.*

Begin with your favorite Induction or use going down Levels A, B, and C.

From now on, from this moment forward, you are (*and you feel*) so much more calm, confident and in control, in control of your thoughts, feelings, actions and reactions... (*Add other positive suggestions you know they want and need.*)

You recognize and realize any time you communicate with me, your voice keeps you very focused on what you need to be focused on. Soon, you are going to travel back in time to the source, the root source of that negative feeling (*say their dominant negative feeling*) so you can move forward with confidence, grace and ease. In a moment, I am going to count backwards from 3 down to 1, and gently snap my fingers. Just allow every number you hear me say to relax you, and deepen you, and when I gently snap my fingers, you will be back in that recent memory, when you felt that feeling. As you go through the scene become aware of what you are thinking and especially what you are feeling and what you believe. Nod your head when you are ready to this... Good.

With the count of 3, double your relaxation, time traveling back in time to that recent memory, 2, double your relaxation, back in time, trusting your first impressions and 1, (*SNAP*) back in that recent scene now... As you go through the scene, heighten your senses, and become aware of what you are thinking, feeling and believe in that scene. Trust your impressions and replay it now... Good. What emotion are you feeling in that scene? ... What do you believe? (*Figuring out what belief they created may take a moment.*)

THE ESSENTIAL 4: HOW TO EFFECTIVELY LEAD YOUR CLIENT TO TAKE CONTROL OF THEIR STATE, THEIR FUTURE & THEIR LIFE

If needed, heighten your senses and replay the scene and notice where you feel that feeling. Is it in your head, your heart, your belly, or all over? Where do you feel that feeling? ... Good. What shape is it? Is it round, globular, square, or pointy? What shape is it? ... Good. What color is that feeling? ... Good. Is it heavy, light, medium, or dense? ... Is it making any sounds or saying anything? ...

(Optional) In a moment, I am going to touch your arm (forearm) and begin counting backwards from 3 down to 1 and gently snap my fingers. With each number you hear me say, amp up that feeling but only as much you can handle and allow your Subconscious Mind to guide you back in time to the root cause, to the source of that feeling, to the first time you ever felt that feeling.

Ready? (*touch arm now*) Amp up that feeling, but only as much as you can handle as you go back in time to the source, with count of 3, trust your first impressions, time traveling back in time with the count of 2, amp up that feeling, traveling back in time now to the root cause, to the source, to the first time you ever felt that feeling and 1, (*SNAP*). Be there now! Trust your impressions. Are you inside or outside? ... Is it daytime or nighttime? ... Are you alone or with others? ... Around what age are you? ... What's happening in this scene? ... What are you feeling? ... What else are you feeling? ... What do you believe?

> *If client is very emotional, immediately bring the adult self into that scene and love up or rescue that younger self to get him/her out of there quickly to a safe place.*

Bring the wiser, loving adult you of today into that scene right now. Do whatever you need to do to help that you in the scene to feel a little better. You might hold 'that younger you,' hug or snuggle and cuddle 'that younger you' ... Let me know when that younger you is feeling a little better... Good.

Talk to 'that younger you' and let 'that you' know that you will always be there for him/her now. He/she is safe now. Tell him/her how beautiful he/she is, how loved he/she is and anything else to help him/her know the truth... that he/she is good enough, always has been, always will be good enough. Keep talking with and loving him/her. Just do whatever it takes to help that you feel better... Nod your head when 'that you' in that scene is feeling better... Good.

> **B.E.R.P. Your Client – Beliefs, Emotions, Resources, Positive learnings**

Now, move in time to right before that scene began. What resources would help you get through that scene so that the memory becomes neutralized or empowering? Do you need courage? ... love? ... strength? ... confidence? Imagine those qualities, those resources flowing into that you, like colors and superpowers being downloaded into that you right now... Nod your head when you have done that... Good.

What belief did that younger you create about yourself or the world? Help that you uncover the beliefs... (*You might need to give some ideas of limiting beliefs.*)

We are going to help 'that you' in that scene know the truth about yourself and feel loved and safe. I am going to play a song so that 'the adult you' of today and that adorable little you can bond. You can sing, dance, hug, bring other people or animals there — do anything you want with 'that you,' while I play this song...

> *Play a Song*
> *"You Are So Beautiful" by Joe Cocker*
> *~ Sing some of the song to them too. ~*

After the song: How's that younger you feeling now? ... Good... And with 'the adult you' helping, is there anything else 'that younger you' or 'the adult you' would like to say or do to neutralize or change that scene? Give a HUG, speak up for yourself, YELL at someone or...? If so, take care of that now and nod your head when you have done that...

Alternative Option 1: Imagine that little you really big and the 'antagonist' smaller, farther away, draining out the color and the sound.

Alternative Option 2: Imagine the 'antagonist' shrinking and becoming a little crying toddler. What would you like to do to that lonely scared little boy/girl?

It's now time for you to become aware of any positive learnings you learned or can now learn from that event. You might need to help that younger you discover or uncover positive learnings. (You might need to give some ideas of positive learnings: *Your broke the pattern. Everyone was doing the best they could. You're okay. You got through it. You're stronger than you thought. You can take care of yourself. You are capable. You'll be okay no matter what happens. It was beyond my abilities to help when I was so young.*)

Now, imagine 'that little you,' that is now filled up with all those resources shrinking down to just the right size to put her in your heart, so you can love 'that little you' and take care of 'that little you' from this moment forward. Nod your head when you have done this... Good.

Now moving forward in time, allow all the memories connected to this event to be healed, re-evaluated and updated, integrating the new resources, new beliefs, and positive learnings into all the memories and subsequent memories linked to this event. Move forward in time now allowing that update, that upgrade and all the positive learning and resources to flow into all the events linked to this event until you:

Get into that recent scene when we began: are in that recent scene when we began. What are you feeling in that recent scene now? What do you believe? Replay that scene now feeling the new feelings, resources, and positive learnings. Go through that scene now so it's neutral or empowering. When you have done that nod your head.

Next most important scene: are in the next most important scene (describe the scene they mentioned — 8 years old, outside, at school) Be in that scene now. What are you feeling in that scene now?

THE ESSENTIAL 4: HOW TO EFFECTIVELY LEAD YOUR CLIENT TO TAKE CONTROL OF THEIR STATE, THEIR FUTURE & THEIR LIFE

> *If they aren't feeling better, have the adult self go into that scene and bring anyone else needed to help that younger self, to reframe the experience.*

When feeling better: Have that scene go differently now. You can shrink that you down and put 'that you' in your heart again, and then continue moving forward in time allowing all the memories connected to this to be healed and re-evaluated until you get back into the recent scene, when we began. Nod your head when you are in that recent scene... What are you feeling in that scene now? (*It should be neutralized or more resourceful.*) ... Continue to move forward in time allowing all the healing, re-evaluating and integrating of the new feelings and beliefs until you are in your future about 1 month from today. Imagine it's 1 month from today... see, hear, feel and experience the evidence of this new you. What's your life like one month from today? ... What's in your life? ... What's not in your life? ... Picture, hear and feel the evidence of these changes. Nod your head when you have done that... Good.

Now go out 6 months from today after making these changes. Imagine your life 6 months from today. Look at that you, feel those positive qualities that make up that future you. Imagine those qualities as colors.

Ask that future you for some wisdom for yourself back at now. What does that future self show you or tell you? ... See, hear and feel that future wisdom now... Good. Now in just a moment you and your future self are going to merge and become one so all the wisdom, all those positive learnings flows right into the you of today into your very DNA. Sense that happening now as you become a team, a dream team working together like a well-oiled machine... Nod your head when you have done that... Good, wonderful.

Now, it's time to come back to now, into a new mind, a new body a new you. Go ahead now and put your hands on your heart. In just moment, say hello to yourself, say your name and say I love you to yourself... Nod your head when you have done that. Good now state one, two or three affirmations that reinforces the new you that is about to emerge...

Good, in a moment, I am going to count from 1 up to 5, when I get to 5 you will open your eyes as a new you. Starting right now with the count of 1, take a big deep energy breathe in, 2, speeding up now into the present, in a new mind, a new body, a new you. 3 another big deep energy breath in of confidence and energy, 4, coming up even more with even more confidence and more energy and with the count of 5 (*SNAP*) open your eyes.

SESSION III
THE TIME LINE THERAPY SESSION

"I've lived through some terrible things in my life, some of which actually happened."

—Mark Twain

THE TIME LINE THERAPY SESSION
– OUTLINE –
PART I

1. *Explain Time Line Therapy.*

    a. Your time line is how you subconsciously store your memories.

    b. "Everyone has a way of mapping and coding time because our minds need to know what we have done and what still needs to get done. So, when we think of our past memories and future memories, we actually store them in different locations."

    c. Explain what memories are — pictures, sounds and feelings. For example, Ask the client to think of a past birthday party. Future memories are also pictures, sounds, and feelings.

    d. Most people store their memories in a line like slides in a slide show, because we have been taught time on a line.

    e. Demonstrate how you code your memories and how others code time, too.

    f. Assure client there is no right or wrong way but that some ways of mapping or coding memories (time) are more resourceful and useful than others.

2. Discovering your client's time line — how they subconsciously map and code time.

    a. Have the client stand up and close their eyes to do this. Make sure there are no obstacles around them so that your client can move forward, backward, left or right, if necessary.

    b. Ask the client to come up with neutral memories to be used as 'markers' to discover where and how the client stores memories. Strong emotional events may not be on their actual time lines.

c. Write down their memories so you can refer to them as needed. It speeds up the processes and helps it run smoothly.

3. Past Memories.

   a. "Choose a neutral memory from yesterday. Got it? In a couple of words, describe the memory. (*Write it down.*) Picture the memory happening, see it, hear it, feel it and notice where you sense it is located. It might be in front of you, to the left, right, behind you or inside of you."

   b. "Where do you sense this memory is located? Point to the memory now... Remember where you are pointing."

   c. "Choose another neutral memory around 1, 2 or 3 years ago. It could be a vacation, a visit from a friend, or when you went out to dinner."

   d. "Using both hands, point to each of the memories. Now, imagine these memories are connected by a line with other memories stored in between like slides in a slide show. Okay?"

   e. "Choose another neutral memory, 10 to 14 years ago, and then point to it."

   f. And another until you and the client have a map of their past time line.

> *If their past time line zigzags in unusual or hard to remember formations consider relocating past time line before discovering their future.*

4. Present and Future Memories.

   a. "Let's see how you map and code your present and your future memories. Think of something you know you have to do tomorrow or over the weekend. Where do you sense that future memory and point to it? Okay, now come up with something you know you will be doing in a few weeks or an upcoming holiday, point to where you sense that's located."

b. Continue getting more memory markers until you get a clear picture of their future time line.

5. Have them connect their Past, Present and Future as one continuous 'line.'

6. Relocating Time Lines.

   a. "Let's check and see if there is a more resourceful and useful way for you to map and code time to help you heal and be the best you can be."

   b. "The way to determine this is to ask your higher self and your Subconscious Mind if there is a more resourceful and useful way for you to map and code time to help you be the best you can be and then start rearranging. Notice how new time lines make you feel. You want to feel a lightness instead of tightness in your belly or heart area. You can keep rearranging until you feel lighter or more at ease."

   c. "You can use your hands or even move your body forward, backward, left or right (*demonstrate*). You might want to start with your youngest memory and stretch it out to make an organized line and see how that feels. Then you can rearrange it so it flows in the direction that feels the best for you."

   d. "Now ask your higher self and your wise Subconscious Mind (or higher power, God) to guide you and help you relocate time in a more resourceful and useful way to help you be the best you can be."

   e. "Keep rearranging until it feels. Nod your head to let me know. If all parts of you agree this will be your new way of mapping and coding time."

   f. Check to see if any traumatic or perceived traumatic memories are in front of their body instead of in their past. If so, do another process with them to move the memory into their past time line and then drop the memory out into a garbage truck and replace it with an empowered self-image. Repeat as needed. (*Make sounds of garbage truck, dropping the memory, etc.*)

THE TIME LINE THERAPY SESSION
— OUTLINE —
PART II

> *In hypnosis, you can ask the client's higher self to help them discover the most important belief for them to release today.*

1. Discuss and get clear on the dominant limiting belief your client would like to resolve and update.

2. Hypnotize client.

3. Choose and confirm limiting belief they are working on releasing and reframing.

4. Ask the client to float above their time line and become the observer, the objective observer.

5. Choose a guide.

6. Ask the client to stay above their time line and float back in time to the root cause of the limiting belief.

7. "Become aware of what age you are, what's happening and why 'that you' created that belief."

8. "Become aware of and preserve any and all positive learnings you can now learn from that event."

9. "Imagine the learnings coming up off the event like a color or energy integrating inside of you for utilization in the future."

THE ESSENTIAL 4: HOW TO EFFECTIVELY LEAD YOUR CLIENT TO TAKE CONTROL OF THEIR STATE, THEIR FUTURE & THEIR LIFE

10. "Float back into your past to no place in particular, just float back until the event is just a pin dot in your future."

11. "As the emotions become neutral let me know they are."

12. "Come back to the event now, and as the emotions become neutral let me know they are."

13. "What resources does 'that you' require in that scene to retain the wisdom to grow up to be the person you are **destined to be to let go of that limiting belief**?" *Suggest options: Love, compassion, courage strength, etc.*

14. "If these and any additional resources you choose to add were a color what color would it be?"

15. "If a symbol could symbolize these resources, which symbol would symbolize them best?"

16. "Float down as your adult self into 'that you,' the resourced you."

17. "Flow a beautiful wave of color and install thousands of those symbols into any and all events related to this one."

18. "As you come back to now allow your subconscious mind to heal the history linked to this event. Float back to now, allowing all the healing, integrating, and re-evaluating of all the events and subsequent events linked to this one. Nod your head when you have reached now."

19. "Go out into your future 1 year from today. See, hear and feel the evidence of these changes."

20. "Go out 5 years from today. What does your future feel like 5 years from today?"

21. "Go out 10 years into your future. What's in your life, what's not in your life? Become aware of all the resources inside of 'that future you.' Ask 'that future you' for some wisdom for yourself back at now. What does your future self tell you? Now you and your future self are a dream team working together like a well-oiled machine."

22. "Now merge with your future self so all the learning and wisdom flows into the you of today into your very DNA."

23. Take the client out of hypnosis.

The Time Line Therapy Session
– Tips & Checklist for Success –

BEFORE HYPNOSIS:

☐ Ask the client, "What went well for you since your last session?"

☐ Discover a limiting belief that would be in your client's best interest to release.

☐ Explain time line. Mapping and coding time is a subconscious process that we are bringing to conscious awareness.

☐ My favorite part of discovering peoples Time Lines is that there is no wrong or right way, but some ways are more resourceful and useful than others. Repeatedly explain this to them so they feel comfortable with the process.

☐ Give examples of various time lines. Include 'in and through' time examples.

☐ Discover your client's time line — how they map and code time. Start with the past.

☐ If necessary, relocate time line to help them be the best they can be.

☐ If needed, move painful memories into the past where they belong.

☐ Then drop the painful memories out of their time line into a garbage truck beneath it. Replace the negative memory with love, light or a resourceful memory, even if it's made up.

DURING HYPNOSIS:

☐ Take them downstairs to a peaceful place.

☐ Confirm the limiting belief they are going to release.

- ☐ Have them float above time line or if needed they go to right or left of time line.
- ☐ Get a guide to go back in time with them. Any guide will do: a dog, a friend, a light, an angel or spirit guide.
- ☐ Make sure they are comfortable with the guide.
- ☐ If it's a deceased ancestor, allow them to spend time with them.
- ☐ Get wisdom from the guide.

AFTER HYPNOSIS:

- ☐ Ask them how they are feeling.
- ☐ Give them homework to go over the forgiveness component in guidebook.

TIME LINE EXAMPLES:

- ☐ In front of them, going from left to right with the past going off to the left and the future going off to the right. This is a common and resourceful way clients map their time line.
- ☐ A 'V' formation with the client in the center of the V with the past veering to the left and the future veering to the right.
- ☐ Past behind them, comes through their body and their future is in front of them.

PREPARING FOR THE UNEXPECTED:

- ☐ Time line can be a difficult process for people to understand.

- ☐ 'In Time' vs. 'Through Time' — 'In Time' clients have time lines that go in their body. That's common but I have noticed at times, the location can be an area holding pain or discomfort.

- ☐ When people recall a memory, it can move out of their time line to right in front of their body.

- ☐ Some people have very unusual ways of mapping and coding time. Help them feel secure about it by letting them know there is no wrong way to experience this. Although some ways are more resourceful and useful.

- ☐ Most ADD & ADHD clients store their memories in a very disorganized way, often in front of them.

TIME LINE HYPNOTIC REGRESSION:

- ☐ If necessary, you can regress the client back to the root cause of the emotion instead of the belief.

- ☐ Sometimes it's important for the client to spend a few moments connecting and talking with their guide. It could be loved one who passed on that they haven't seen in a long time.

- ☐ If your client is having trouble being above the body, suggest they go off to one side instead.

- ☐ Sometimes your client will need to become more associated with the experience. Allow it and help them along like you did in the first regression session.

THE TIME LINE THERAPY SESSION
— SCRIPT —

Begin with your favorite Induction or downstairs to Peaceful Place or their Superpowers Place or both. Deliver positive suggestions and get clear on the limiting belief you client is going to release today.

Very soon indeed your subconscious mind and your higher self are going to take you back in time to the event — to the experience — when that limiting belief began. Right now get clear on the limiting belief you would like to get to the root cause of and release today. Nod your head when you are clear... Good. Go ahead and tell me what that limiting belief is... Wonderful. In just a moment, you are going to go back in time to the root cause, to the source to the event when that limiting belief began so that you can heal and transform your past, present and your future. Just trust and allow your subconscious mind and your higher self (God) to make it easy for you to access the information you need to release that limiting belief.

Begin to sense your time line and where it is now located. Imagine your past now and realize it's connected by a thread of emotions, to a belief about yourself.

Begin to imagine that spiritual you, the observer, lifting right above the body... getting lighter, and lighter, and lighter. Become the observer, objective observer. Nod your head when you sense you are above your body... Good. Now, notice your time lines stretching off in the directions that you do now.

In a moment, you will have the opportunity to invite in a guide, a mentor, or an angelic presence, to travel with you back in time. Just trust your impressions. I will count from 3 down to 1 and gently snap my fingers. Allow each number to relax you and deepen you and when I gently snap my fingers, invite in a guide, a mentor or an angelic presence to travel with you back in time. Nod your head when you are ready to do this... Good.

THE ESSENTIAL 4: HOW TO EFFECTIVELY LEAD YOUR CLIENT TO TAKE CONTROL OF THEIR STATE, THEIR FUTURE & THEIR LIFE

With the count of 3, double your relaxation, 2, even deeper now, trusting your impressions and, 1, invite in a guide now (*SNAP*)... Nod your head when you see, hear or feel, a presence... Good. Do you feel comfortable around this being...? Do you know who it is...?

- **Yes:** Good, go ahead and connect with your guide and ask for some wisdom.

- **No:** Ask your guide what he or she likes to be called. Trust the name you get and then ask for some wisdom.

Nod your head when you have done that... Wonderful. Now it's time to give your full focus to your past, sensing your past down below. In a moment I am going to count from 3 down to 1 and gently snap my fingers. Allow every number to relax you and deepen you and by the time I snap my fingers you and your guide will travel back in time to the root cause of that belief. Ready? Give your full focus towards the past, sensing the past down below, invite your subconscious mind, your higher self, and your guide to take you back in time now to the root cause of that belief, 3 begin time traveling back in time 2, going back in time, trusting your first impressions and, 1, be there now (*SNAP*) above that event. Nod your head when you sense you have arrived... As you look down at that event, become aware of what age you are, what's happening in that scene, and why 'that you' created this belief.

Ask your subconscious mind and higher self to become aware of and preserve any and all the positive learnings you can now learn from this event. Become aware of any wisdom, clarity, or compassion you can experience or learn right now? (*You might need to help them discover positive learnings.*) Nod your head when you have those positive learnings... Imagine those positive learnings coming up off that event like a color, or colors, or energy integrating inside of you for your utilization in the future... Nod your head when you have done that... Good.

Allow 'that you,' with all the positive learnings inside, to move further back into your past. Just go further back and further back to no place in particular. Just go further back into your past until that event is just a pin dot in your future... Nod your head when you have done that... Good.

Being before the event notice that the emotions become neutral, and as they are, let me know they are... Good. Come back to that event and look down at that event and notice that the emotions are neutral, and as they are let me know they are... Good.

What resources or qualities does 'that you' in the scene require to retain the wisdom to grow to be the person you are destined to be, to let go of that limiting belief? Does 'that you' require love, strength, compassion, confidence, courage...? If these and any additional resources you choose to add were a color or colors, become aware of those colors now... And if a symbol could symbolize these resources what symbol would symbolize them best?

I ask you now to flow an infinite river of color or colors into 'that you' in the scene and fill every cell in your body until you are flooded inside with these resources. Let me know when 'that you' in the scene feels fully resourced and looks, sounds and feels great.

Float down as your adult self into that you that is now filled with all these resources. Invite that you, that is now healed to integrate inside of the you of today. Nod your head when you have done that... Good.

Rise above that event and flow a beautiful wave of color or colors and install 1000's of those symbols into any and all events related to this one, healing, integrating and evolving every one of the events, and all the subsequent events linked to this event, all the way back to now. As you float back to now, allow your subconscious mind to heal the history linked to this event — begin coming back to now only as quickly as your subconscious mind can heal, integrate, re-evaluate and update all events linked to this one. Nod your head when you have reached now... Good.

> *Remember to add suggestions related to your client's beliefs.*

THE ESSENTIAL 4: HOW TO EFFECTIVELY LEAD YOUR CLIENT TO TAKE CONTROL OF THEIR STATE, THEIR FUTURE & THEIR LIFE

Now go out into your future, give your full focus towards your future. Go out 1 year from today. Having made these changes today and from all our work together, how does your future look, sound and feel a year from today? What's in your life? What's not in your life? See, hear and feel the evidence of our work together... Nod your head when you have done that... Good.

Now go out 5 years from today. Imagine yourself 5 years from today. How does your life feel 5 years from today? What's in your life? What's not in your life? See, hear and feel the evidence of our work together... Nod your head when you have done that... Good.

Now go out 10 years from today. Experience your future self, 10 years from today. How does your life feel 10 years from today? What's in your life? What's not in your life? See, hear and feel the evidence of our work together... Nod your head when you have done that... Good.

What qualities and resources make up that future you? Become aware of those resources and picture them like colors or symbols inside of 'that future you.'

Ask 'that future you' for some wisdom for yourself back at now. What does your future self show you or tell you? Good. Now celebrate with your future self. High five, hug, or any other way you like to celebrate because your future self is very grateful for the work you are doing today. In just a moment you and your future self are going to merge so all those resources and all the wisdom of 10 years of insights flow into the you of today into your very DNA. Merge with your future self now. Nod your head when you have done this... Good.

Now it's time for you to come back to now, float back to now with all the wisdom and resources inside of you. Put your hands on your heart and say hello to yourself. Say your name and say I love you. Then state one, two or three positive affirmations, that reinforces the new you that is about to emerge. (*Make sure it's related to the belief, keeping it positive. You may need to give them some ideas of affirmations.*)

Once you have the affirmation, state it out loud. Now state it out loud about five times in a row, no need to count, just state your affirmation five times right now. (*Again, make sure it's in the positive tense and at least one of their statements is an "I am" statement. You can also say it with them.*)

In a moment, I am going to count from 1 up to 5, and gently snap my fingers, when I snap my fingers, this new you will emerge, with new beliefs about yourself, your life, and your future. Starting right now with the count of 1, take a big, deep, energy breath in, 2, speeding up now with lots of confidence and energy, 3, into the present in a new mind, a new body, a new you. 4 coming up even more, with more confidence and more energy, and with the count of 5 (*SNAP*) open your eyes.

SESSION IV
THE FORGIVENESS FIRE™ SESSION

"Resenting another human being is like drinking poison and expecting someone else to be sick."

—Tony Robbins

THE FORGIVENESS FIRE™ SESSION
— OUTLINE —

1. Explain the process and ask client, "What do you think forgiveness is?" and "What do you think forgiveness does?" (*Write down the answers to read to them at The Forgiveness Fire™.*)

2. Induction — Have the client set their intentions during the induction.

3. Have the client invite in a Guide, Mentor, or Angelic Presence to go to The Forgiveness Fire with them.

4. Walk the client to the entrance of the *Welcoming Woods / Friendly Forest*.

5. Utilize the HeartMath Breathing Technique to open their heart and prepare them for forgiveness.

6. Journey through the woods towards the meadow to the Forgiveness Fire™.

7. Have the client take a moment to connect with the Forgiveness Fire™. (*Offer gratitude.*)

8. Deepen the client's understanding of forgiveness by sharing insights into the benefits. Make sure to also say *what the client said forgiveness is and does*.

9. Invite people to come to the fire — (approximately 3 times)

    a. Ask the client to communicate from their heart what he/she has been wanting or needing to say.

    b. Have the person who came respond to what was said by the client, and also share what he/she has been wanting or needing to say.

    c. Continue communicating and saying and doing everything that needs to be said and done.

10. Check for cords.

    a. Don't check for cords when it is a part of the client that arrives, instead merge.

    b. Sever cords to take back their power and soul fragments (memories)

    c. Create a new one heart to heart with Source. (Optional.)

11. Recite the Ho'oponopono prayer four times. Have the client say it to the person there or have that person say it to your client or both or neither.

12. Connect with Source, Light, God so that unconditional love is flowing into the client and into the person and into their hearts as unconditional love.

13. Future Pace.

14. Take them out of hypnosis.

THE FORGIVENESS FIRE™ SESSION
– TIPS & CHECKLIST FOR SUCCESS –

BEFORE HYPNOSIS:

☐ Ask the client, "What went well for you since the last time I saw you?"

☐ Ask them specific questions and use their answers during the session:
- "What do you think forgiveness is?"
- "What do you think forgiveness does?"
- "Are you willing to forgive?"
- "Are you ready to forgive?"

☐ Explain The Forgiveness Fire™ process to the client.
- "Anyone who needs to forgive you, or you need to forgive, or both, including yourself, a situation or someone who's passed on can come to The Forgiveness Fire™."
- "Everyone who comes to The Forgiveness Fire™ comes with an open heart and communicates from their heart so new things can be seen, felt heard, understood as well as healed and released."
- Also explain that the communications come from a higher place. Higher self to higher self instead of the ego self to ego self.
- The Forgiveness Fire exists in a meadow.
- The Forgiveness Fire transcends space and time.

☐ Determine if the client is ready for forgiveness.
- If not, that's okay, just do more confidence building, ego strengthening and emotional clearing until the client is ready for the session.
    — Are you ready to forgive?
    — Are you willing to forgive?

THE ESSENTIAL 4: HOW TO EFFECTIVELY LEAD YOUR CLIENT TO TAKE CONTROL OF THEIR STATE, THEIR FUTURE & THEIR LIFE

- [ ] Ask them these specific questions and use their answers during the session:
    - "What do you think forgiveness is?"
    - "What do you think forgiveness does?"

DURING HYPNOSIS:

- [ ] The client may choose to go to the fire without a guide, that's fine as it may be more empowering for them.

- [ ] Due to fears and other factors, you may have to help the client invite specific people to the fire, including inviting a part of themselves.

- [ ] It's usually very important that the client has an opportunity to communicate with a 'part' of himself or herself. You may have to invite a part of the client to the fire for them.

- [ ] You can have the client communicate out loud or in their minds. Just make sure the client is on track with forgiving, letting go and neutralizing.

PREPARING FOR THE UNEXPECTED:

- [ ] The client may choose to go to the fire without a guide.

- [ ] You may have to help them invite specific people including themselves to the fire.

- [ ] Ancestors who have passed on may come to say hello and give messages.

- [ ] Some people need more emotional and belief clearing before they are ready to forgive on the 4th session.

- [ ] Keep a heart to heart cord but severing all the other cords is ideal because it gives the client a chance to get back soul fragments — from memories.

THE FORGIVENESS FIRE™ SESSION
— SCRIPT —

Begin with your favorite induction or dissolving numbers in the sand of 5, 4, 3, 2, 1...

Allow every step you take to relax you and deepen you. Listen for any animals there welcoming you greeting you. Just allow yourself to relax, and let go, and drift down deeper, and deeper to that place inside you where things change, where things heal, where insight lives. Good. You are feeling good, really good now, because you know that you realize you are continuing to free yourself of old patterns, of old beliefs, of those old negative feelings that no longer serve you. It's time to be free and allow yourself to become an even better version of your best self.

The Forgiveness Fire is a sacred fire that transcends all time and space; anyone you need to forgive or needs to forgive you, or both, including yourself, a situation, or even someone who has already passed on, can come to the forgiveness fire for healing.

Feeling relaxed, and at ease. It's time now for you to set your intentions. When you set your intentions, you naturally establish a target so your subconscious mind, your higher self and the Universe (God) knows exactly what you want. How do you want to feel after you leave here today? What do you want to have, be, feel, experience, learn or achieve for yourself and your life? Become aware of the results, the desired outcomes you would like to experience. Set your intentions and nod your head when you have done that... Good.

In a moment, you will have the opportunity to invite in a guide, a mentor, or even an angelic presence to go with you to the Forgiveness Fire™. I am going to count backwards from 3 down to 1 and gently snap my fingers, just allow each number you hear me say to relax, and deepen you, and when I gently snap my fingers, invite in a guide, a mentor, or an angelic presence, to go with you to the Forgiveness Fire. Nod your head when you are ready to invite in a guide... Good...

With the count of, 3, Double that relaxation and trust your impressions, 2, — go deeper and deeper into that relaxation and, 1 (*SNAP*) — invite in a guide, mentor, or angelic presence now. Nod your head when you sense, hear or feel a presence... Good.

> *Keep in mind that sometimes the client needs help connecting or even creating a guide and sometimes they need to go to the fire on their own.*

Welcome and greet your guide. Thank them for coming. If you don't know who it is, ask your guide what they like to be called, trust your impressions and let me know... Good. From this moment forward, whenever you communicate with me, your voice will keep you very focused on what you need to be focused on. If your guide has some wisdom for you, ask for that wisdom now, and nod your head when you are done... Good.

(Optional) You can also ask your guide for a signal so that you know when they are around you, guiding you. This signal could be a color, a touch on the shoulder, a breeze, or a specific animal sighting... just ask and trust your impressions. Nod your head when you have done that... Good.

> *If it is a loved one they haven't seen in awhile let them spend some time together reuniting.*

Feeling safe and supported, it's time now for you to go to The Forgiveness Fire. Look over in the distance and become aware of the welcoming woods, the friendly forest. There is a path that will lead you to the meadow where The Forgiveness Fire lives. Walk over to the welcoming woods now and when you arrive at the beginning of the path, stop and nod your head.

Remember now that everyone who goes to the sacred fire, and comes to the fire, must come with an open heart... and communicate from their heart, so new information and wisdom can be seen, felt and heard. It's higher self to higher self so you can get new understandings, and new insights. You too must communicate from you heart. It's easy for you to open your heart and communicate from your heart. Just begin to imagine that you are breathing in, and out, through your heart right now. Imagine that as you breathe in, you are breathing in through your heart (*Say as client breathes in*) and as you breathe out, imagine you are breathing out through your heart. (*Say when client is breathing out*) ... Good... As you focus your breathing on your heart, you activate your heart's intelligence. Activate your heart's intelligence now by continuing to imagine you are breathing in and out through your heart. Now imagine that you are breathing in and out a loving energy, or a loving color, breathing in love and out love so love is in you and surrounding you.

In just a moment, invite your heart to open, and then see, hear, and feel it opening, like a rose bud opening into a beautiful red or purple rose, or a door opening, a tunnel flowing, or a vortex spinning. Invite your heart to open now... and see, hear and feel your heart opening... and then breathe in love and out love, unconditional love, universal love, so love is in you and surrounding you.

To amplify the loving feeling even more, all you need to do is go back to a moment in your life when you felt very loving or very loved or both. Choose a moment in your life when you felt very loving or very loved or both. It could have been yesterday or many years ago. Perhaps in that loving memory you were petting an animal, listening to music, dancing or holding someone or being held. Choose a memory now when you felt very loving, loved or both. Nod your head when you have chosen that loving memory... Good.

In a moment, I am going to count backwards from 3 down to 1 and gently snap my fingers. Just allow every number you hear me say to relax you, and deepen you, and take you back in time to relive that loving memory. When I gently snap my fingers, you'll be back at that event to relive it, so you can connect with that loving feeling and breathe it into your heart and every cell of your entire being. Make it big, and bright, and lifelike, so you can capture and feel that wonderful loving feeling. Nod your head when you are ready... Starting with, 3, going deeper, trust... 2, even deeper, and time traveling back in time to that loving memory and,

THE ESSENTIAL 4: HOW TO EFFECTIVELY LEAD YOUR CLIENT TO TAKE CONTROL OF THEIR STATE, THEIR FUTURE & THEIR LIFE

1 (*SNAP*) be in that event now. Relive it and experience all the details. See, hear, and feel that loving feeling, and breathe it... in... and... out... of your heart... Make the memory bigger, and brighter, and replay it again, and again, to connect with that unconditional loving feeling, that universal loving feeling, that state, that vibration that we call love, unconditional love, universal love. Feel it now and breathe this love into every cell of your entire being... Nod your head when you have done that... Good.

Now you are ready to go to the Forgiveness Fire. With gratitude, trust, and love, imagine you and your guide walking on the path, through the friendly forest, to the Forgiveness Fire. Notice all the beautiful plants and animals surrounding you as you journey through the woods. Become aware of any patches of lush green mosses; beautiful and unusual colored flowers. Notice any tall, magical, and majestic trees. Look, and listen for animals that are welcoming you, and greeting you... Allow each step you take to relax you, and deepen you, and prepare you, for the ultimate healing — forgiveness.

Become aware now, of a clearing in the distance. Perhaps you can already hear the crackling of the fire and see the orange and blue flames. You might be able to smell the burning of the wood at the fire. As you get closer to the meadow, the fire becomes bright, and clear, and welcoming.

Go to the fire now, and feel its warmth, its comfort, its gifts. For this is a sacred fire that transcends all time and space. As you connect with the fire, allow my voice to deepen you, and every breath you breathe... in... and... out... to relax you. Communicate now whatever you would like to say to the fire. Nod your head when you have done that... Good.

> *Include what the client said forgiveness is and what forgiveness does, some important key elements, and components of forgiving... as well as the purpose of forgiving.*

THE ESSENTIAL 4: HOW TO EFFECTIVELY LEAD YOUR CLIENT TO TAKE CONTROL OF THEIR STATE, THEIR FUTURE & THEIR LIFE

Your Subconscious Mind is now ready to hear these statements. You recognize and realize that forgiveness is such an important experience, because when we forgive ourselves, and when we forgive others, we release negative emotional states from our thoughts, our behaviors, our actions, and our reactions. Forgiveness is a feeling in your heart, in the intelligence of your heart, that truly understands you, and knows how to help you be the best you can be. Forgiveness is a deep, and lasting feeling, that forever frees you of negativity. Forgiveness frees you of doubt, worry, guilt, and anger, and (include whatever emotion they are working on releasing). Forgiveness is a divine, highly intelligent, feeling that manifests as healing. Freeing you, releasing you. Releasing your old negative thoughts, releasing your old patterns of behaviors, freeing you to be filled up with divine wisdom, and divine power, and divine love.

> *I usually offer the client a chance to bring someone to the fire approximately 3 times — with the option each time because it can be draining. Sometimes parents will come together. Sometimes an entire family may come, just allow your client to experience it however they need to and guide them along.*

In a moment I am going to count backwards from 3 down to 1 and gently snap my fingers, when I snap my fingers allow your higher self, and your guide to bring the first, most important, person or people for you to forgive, or to forgive you, or both. You just set that invitation out there and trust your impressions. Nod your head when you are ready... With the count of 3, go deeper and trust... 2 relax, go deeper, and trust, and 1 (*SNAP*) invite in the first most important person now. Nod your head when you sense a presence coming towards you... Good. Who's there with you now?

If it is a 'part' of the client — proceed like this: Welcome, and greet this you, and thank this part for coming here today. Around what age do you sense this part is? Older, younger, same age? ... Begin communicating what you would like to say to this you, from your heart, something you may have needed to say for a long time... or perhaps something this you has been needing to hear for a long time. Share from your heart, and listen with your heart, so you can understand 'this you.'

Nod your head when you have done that... Make sure 'this you' has an opportunity to respond in a way that creates clarity and understanding... Go ahead and respond to what 'this you' has said and say anything else that comes up. Just keep communicating until everything that needs to be said or done is said and done. Nod your head when both of you are feeling loved, safe, and good... really good.

In a moment, I am going to recite the Ho'oponopono prayer four times. Take a moment now to say these words to 'that you' or imagine 'that you' saying it to you or both...

I am sorry. Please forgive me. Thank you. I love you.

I am sorry. Please forgive me. Thank you. I love you.

I am sorry. Please forgive me. Thank you. I love you.

I am sorry. Please forgive me. Thank you. I love you.

Now imagine 'that you' and the you of today merging as one, working as a team, filled with love, and strength, and courage... Good. Now go to the fire, and connect with its peace and warmth. Nod your head when you are ready to invite the next most important person for you to forgive, or to forgive you, or both... Good.

Starting with the count of 3, go deeper and trust... 2 double your relaxation, and 1 (*SNAP*) invite in the next most important person for your healing now. Nod your head when you sense a presence coming towards you... Good. Who's there with you now?

If it is anyone else — proceed like this: Welcome, and greet that person, and thank them for coming here today. Imagine that their higher self, their best self, is with you now... Begin communicating from your heart, what you have needed to say, or wanted to say, for a long time. Nod your head when you have done that... Good. Now listen to their response... and listen to what they have been needing to say and wanting to say... Good. Now respond to what they said and say anything else you need to say to allow more healing, clarity, and understanding...

Listen to their response so you can see a new perspective. If there is anything else you would like to say, say it now. Nod your head when you have both said everything that needs to be said and done everything that needs to be done... Good.

> *I keep asking the client to communicate with their visitor until all that is needed to be said and done is said and done. You may need to help them along or confirm that a new awareness is being formed by asking them, "What's happening now?"*

ONLY IF IS NOT A 'PART' OF THEM, CONTINUE THIS WAY:

In a moment, I am going to count down from 3 down to 1 and gently snap my fingers, each number will relax you, and deepen you, when I gently snap my fingers, become aware of any cord or cords coming out of your body as well as where the cords are coming out of you and where they are going into their body. Also become aware of any cord or cords coming out of their body and where they are coming out of their body and where they are going to yours. Nod your head when you are ready... Good. Starting with the count of 3, go deeper and trust, 2, even deeper now, trust your impressions and 1 (*SNAP*) become aware now of any cord or cords coming out of your body, and where they are coming out of your body, and where they are going into their body. Sense any cord or cords now, and tell me where the first cord is coming out of your body... Good... And where is this cord going into their body? ... Good. Notice the size, the shape, textures, and colors of this cord. What color is the cord? ... Is it flowing, stagnate or both? ...

Are there any other cords? Become aware of them now. Is there another cord coming out of your body and going into theirs, or coming out of their body going into yours?

THE ESSENTIAL 4: HOW TO EFFECTIVELY LEAD YOUR CLIENT TO TAKE CONTROL OF THEIR STATE, THEIR FUTURE & THEIR LIFE

If yes continue with the same line of questioning. Sense any cord or cords now, and tell me where the cord is coming out of your body... Good... And where is this cord going into their body? ... Good. Notice the size, the shape, textures, and colors of this cord. What color is the cord? ... Is it flowing, stagnate or both? ... Are there any other cords?

> *If needed write down where the cords are located and other details. Have the client focus on one cord at a time and ask them to notice, the size, shape, color, texture, flowing, stagnate or both. I am especially concerned with color and flowing, stagnate.*

You have 4 choices; choose what's best for you.

1 – You can relocate the cords, so they become one cord, flowing heart to heart, or

2 – You can sever the cords completely, feel the release and take back your power and all your soul fragments, or

3 – You can sever them completely and then create a new one heart to heart.

4 – You can sever them completely and leave them severed.

Choose now what's best for you. Do you need to sever the cords completely? Or do you want to sever them and then create a fresh new one, heart to heart? Let me know what you are choosing to do... Good.

SEVER CORDS: Now choose how you are going to sever the cords, what tool do you need — knife, a machete, or scissors? Or maybe you just unhook the cords. Go ahead and unhook or sever the cord(s) and sense that release, your power and soul fragments from past memories coming back into you. (*Client may not feel this — that's okay.*)

RELOCATE CORDS: Go ahead now and begin to organize and relocate the cords so they become one cord, coming out of your heart, and flowing into their heart, and back into your heart. Once you have done that; begin to sense the color changing, adding a greenish or pinkish glow to the cord as it flows back and forth, heart to heart.

Now begin to imagine a white light coming from up above... from a central point, from the source of all that is (*God, Creator, Universe — use their words*) and imagine this light is filled with unconditional and universal love. Imagine the light and love flowing down into the top of your head, through your head, your throat, and into your heart. Sense the light coming out of your heart and flowing into (*name of person there e.g., Your mother, sister, or the actual name*). At the same time, picture that light coming down from [*the Source*] into (*name of person there e.g., Your mother, sister, or the actual name*) head and down through their head, throat, and into their heart. See it flowing out of their heart, into your heart, flowing up from your heart through your head up to [*the Source*], and then flowing back down into both of your heads and hearts forming a triangle of universal, unconditional love. Nod your head when you have done this... Wonderful.

As you sense this unconditional love, universal love and forgiveness flowing. I am going to recite the Ho'oponopono prayer four times. You can say it to them. Or they can say it to you, or both, or neither. If it's for your highest good, say these words to 'that you' or imagine 'that you' saying them to you or both or neither...

I am sorry. Please forgive me. Thank you. I love you.

I am sorry. Please forgive me. Thank you. I love you.

I am sorry. Please forgive me. Thank you. I love you.

I am sorry. Please forgive me. Thank you. I love you.

You have a choice now to invite (*name of person there e.g., Your mother, sister, or the actual name*) to stay with you by the fire or have them go back to where they came from. Do what's best for you... and then go to the fire and connect with the fire as you feel its warmth. Feel it's comfort as you just allow yourself to relax and go deeper and prepare yourself for the next most important

THE ESSENTIAL 4: HOW TO EFFECTIVELY LEAD YOUR CLIENT TO TAKE CONTROL OF THEIR STATE, THEIR FUTURE & THEIR LIFE

person you need to forgive, or needs to forgive you, or both. Nod your head when you are ready to invite in the next most important person or people... Good.

With the count of 3, go deeper, 2 even deeper now, and 1, (*SNAP*) let me know who's coming toward you now.

> *Repeat the process of communication, cords, Unconditional love flowing from source and the Ho'oponopono prayer — After about 3 times — sometimes more and sometimes less, the client is usually ready to be done and you may be out of time.*

As you stand by the fire now, begin to look on the other side of the fire at your future self. Imagine and sense your future self there now, healed and free. Look closely at this you who has made these changes today. What's this future you thinking and feeling? ... How does this future you communicate? ... See and feel the evidence of having made these changes today in that future you... What qualities are inside you? ... What do you no longer carry with you?

Is {*the fear, the weight*} gone? ... What is it replaced with? ... Strength? ... Courage? ... Confidence? ... Acceptance? ... Go over to 'that you,' hug 'that you,' honor and celebrate with your future self now... Ask for a message from your future self for the self back at now. Become aware of that message now... Let this message flow into every cell of your entire being. As you imagine 'this future you' notice the qualities, the resources that are a part of 'this future you,' as if they are a color or energy or power. See and feel them in that you... Merge with 'that future you' so all the qualities, knowledge, wisdom, and resources flow inside of 'the you of today,' into your very DNA. Nod your head when you have done that... Good.

Now thank the fire, your higher self, your guide, and anyone else you would like to thank... Good. Now begin walking towards the friendly forest with lightness, and a peace that stays with you from this moment forward.

In a moment I am going to count from 1 up to 5, when I get to 5 a new you will emerge, with new beliefs about yourself, your life and your future. Starting with the count of 1, take a big, deep, energy breath in, 2, speeding up now with lots of confidence and energy, 3, into the present, into a new mind, a new body, a new you. 4, coming up even more, with more confidence and energy, and with the count of 5 (*SNAP*) open your eyes.

POSITIVE & NEGATIVE FEELINGS, EMOTIONS, AND BELIEFS

Positive Feelings, Emotions & Beliefs

Peace	Joy	Driven
Love	Caring	Spiritual
Strength	Compassionate	Connected
Courage	Forgiving	Empowered
Confidence	Passion	Powerful
Curiosity	Calm	Flexible
Trust	Balanced	Serenity
Patience	Capable	Organized
Resourceful	Determined	
Acceptance	Motivated	

I am enough.
I am good enough.
I am loved enough.

I am strong enough.
I am smart enough.
I am creative enough.

Negative Feelings, Emotions & Beliefs

Frustration	Insecurity	Shame
Doubt	Overwhelmed	Bored
Worry	Resentment	Dread
Annoyed	Rejection	Judgment
Anger	Regret	Envy
Guilt	Stuck	Perfectionism
Fear	Stressed	Self-Conscious
Pain	Jealous	Defeat
Depression	Confusion	Embarrassed
Anxiety	Procrastination	

I am not enough.
I am not loved enough.
I am not strong enough.

I am not creative enough.
I am not smart enough.

Common Limiting Beliefs

I'm not good enough.

I am not enough.
I am not good enough.
I am not loved enough.
I am not strong enough.
I am not creative enough.
I am not smart enough.

Other Beliefs

I'll always feel this way.
I'll never find love.
I'll always be alone.
I'll never have enough money.
There's something wrong with me.
I'll never heal.
I'll never lose the weight.

The HeartMath Breathing Technique

Create a coherent state in about a minute with these simple but powerful steps.

Step 1 Heart Breathing — focus your attention on your heart, as if you are breathing in and out through your heart. As you breathe, imagine as if you are breathing in and out through your heart. You can rhythmically breathe or deep breathe, just focus your breathing on your heart.

Step 2 Open Your Heart — continue to breathe as if you are breathing in and out through your heart. Now invite your heart to open and then see, hear and feel it opening perhaps like a rosebud opening into a beautiful purple or red rose or perhaps like a door opening, tunnel flowing or vortex spinning. Now with your heart open, imagine that you are breathing in love in out love (or joy or appreciation) so love is in you and around you.

Step 3 Activate a wonderful feeling — To amplify a wonderful feeling, choose a memory when you felt very loving, loved or both. It could have been yesterday or many years ago. Your loving memory could have been petting an animal or holding someone or being held. Choose that memory now and soon you will time travel back to that memory to relive the memory, feel the loving feeling and breathe it in and out through your heart.

Source: HeartMath LLC, www.heartmath.com/quick-coherence-technique

THE HO'OPONOPONO PRAYER

I'm Sorry.
Please Forgive Me.
Thank You.
I love you.

Ho'oponopono is a Hawaiian healing practice. It means "to make things right." By feeling and saying the words "I'm sorry, I love you, please forgive me, I thank you," we take responsibility for ourselves and the world we create.

By clearing ourselves with love, forgiveness and gratitude we clear the experiences of the past, present and future. The words with intention are vibrations that break up old patterns of fear and negativity.

Ho'oponopono is personal and universal. When we get in touch with our deepest feelings of compassion, forgiveness and gratitude for ourselves there is great healing. We then have the capacity to love and heal others.

To forgive ourselves or those who hurt us opens the heart and allows us to love more.

These words, "I'm sorry, I love you, please forgive me, I thank you" are so powerful. They heal the collective. We feel or move towards feeling forgiveness, compassion, love and gratitude for all life and all that has happened.

I like to sing. It is the language of the heart. It opens up the breath and moves energy up and out. Singing, making sounds, laughing, crying release stagnant energy and emotions and break up old patterns that no longer serve us.

When chanting Ho'oponopono I feel I am being breathed by the breath of spirit and sung by the song of life.

Source: www.wanttoknow.info/070701imsorryiloveyoujoevitale